WOMEN SPORTS STARS

Maya Moore
Basketball Star

by Lori Mortensen

CAPSTONE PRESS
a capstone imprint

Snap Books are published by Capstone Press,
1710 Roe Crest Drive, North Mankato, Minnesota 56003
www.mycapstone.com

Library of Congress Cataloging-in-Publication Data
Names: Mortensen, Lori, 1955- author.
Title: Maya Moore : basketball star / by Lori Mortensen.
Description: North Mankato, Minnesota : An imprint of Capstone Press, [2018]
  | Series: Snap Books. Women Sports Stars. | Includes bibliographical
  references and index. | Audience: Ages: 8-14.
Identifiers: LCCN 2017039227 (print) | LCCN 2017048700 (ebook) | ISBN
  9781515797173 (eBook PDF) | ISBN 9781515797098 (hardcover) | ISBN
  9781515797135 (paperback)
Subjects: LCSH: Moore, Maya—Juvenile literature. | Basketball players—
  United States—Biography—Juvenile literature. | Women basketball
  players—United States—Biography—Juvenile literature.
Classification: LCC GV884.M635 (ebook) | LCC GV884.M635 M67 2018 (print) |
  DDC 796.323092 [B] –dc23
LC record available at https://lccn.loc.gov/2017039227

Editorial Credits
Abby Colich, editor; Kayla Rossow, designer; Eric Gohl, media researcher;
Katy LaVigne, production specialist

Printed and bound in the USA.
010780S18

Table of Contents

CHAPTER 1

Relentless

Maya Moore and the Minnesota Lynx were playing against the Phoenix Mercury. It was a critical game. Whoever won this game would earn a spot in the 2015 WNBA Finals. The Lynx were at a disadvantage. This was the Mercury's home turf. The crowd was on their side. None of that mattered to Maya. She only had one goal — winning.

By the second half, Maya appeared drained, but she kept going. Then she made her move. A quick steal and layup widened the Lynx's narrow lead to 65–62. Minutes later, the Mercury surged up nine points to the Lynx's lackluster four. The score was now 69–71. Moore racked up two free throws. Now the score was tied at 71. Just 38.7 seconds were left.

Maya dribbles the ball in a game against the Phoenix Mercury during a WNBA playoff game in 2015.

FACT

When Maya jumps, she gets lots of air. She has a vertical leap of 26 inches (0.66 meters). That's nearly as high as the average NBA player's vertical leap.

Crunch Time

Whatever happened next would decide the game. Some players buckle under pressure. Not Maya. It was crunch time. That's when she plays her best.

The Mercury had the ball. In a flash, Maya anticipated their pass and deflected it. Players scrambled for the ball. Maya was fouled. Now with only 1.5 seconds left, Maya stood at the free throw line. Would she make her one free throw shot? The entire game rested on her shoulders.

Maya dribbled three times. Then she hurled the ball into the air. Wham! It dropped into the hoop. At the last possible second, Maya gave the Lynx a 72–71 victory.

Maya celebrates the 2015 WNBA championship game win with two teammates.

Maya scored 40 points in one game. That was a playoff record. The Lynx got to the WNBA Finals. They went on to win the 2015 championship.

Winning was nothing new for Maya. Her list of accomplishments includes two college national championships. She's won four WNBA titles. There are also three Chinese league championships and two Olympic gold medals. Maya Moore is the most decorated women's basketball player ever.

WINNING ROUTINE

Maya is not superstitious, but she does follow a routine before a game. She likes to listen to music on the bus or in the car on her way there. "All I Need Is You" by Lecrae, "Take Me to the King" by Tamela Mann, and "Sweet Victory" by Trip Lee are a few favorites from her "gospel-hip hop mix."

CHAPTER 2

Childhood Hoops

Maya's journey to basketball stardom began June 11, 1989. She was born in Jefferson City, Missouri. Maya lived with her mother in a small apartment. Her mother named her after writer Maya Angelou. Growing up, Maya didn't know her father. He was Mike Dabney, a former Rutgers basketball star. He left before she was born. Maya has met him, but she doesn't like to talk about him.

As a kid Maya was always in motion. To burn some of that energy, her mother kept her involved in a lot of activities. Maya especially liked shooting a ball into a mini hoop that hung on the back of a door. Three-year-old Maya spent hours racing down the hallway and dropping shots through the hoop.

When Maya was 8 years old, she got a new basketball hoop — the kind with sand in the bottom. She spent hours in the driveway. She worked on her layups, three-pointers, and free throws. If she bounced the ball off the curb just right, she could grab it midair and drop an awesome alley-oop. Wham!

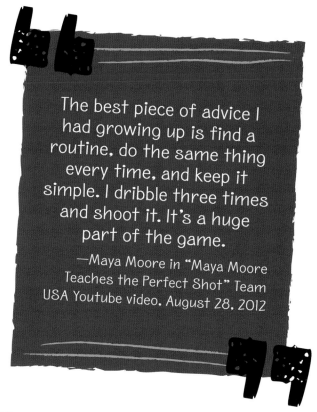

The best piece of advice I had growing up is find a routine, do the same thing every time, and keep it simple. I dribble three times and shoot it. It's a huge part of the game.

—Maya Moore in "Maya Moore Teaches the Perfect Shot" Team USA Youtube video, August 28, 2012

Maya hugs her mom after a game in 2011.

FACT

Maya is also a talented drummer. When she was 10, she started Maya's Mobile Car Wash to earn money for a drum set. She still plays today.

Research and Résumés

In 1996 the WNBA signed its first players. It was about the same time Maya got her basketball hoop. Maya loved watching the women battle it out on TV. They showed her what was possible.

When Maya was 11, she and her mom moved to Charlotte, North Carolina. Her mother started a new job at a phone company. A year later, they moved to Atlanta, Georgia, where her mother worked at a bank.

Although home life was good, middle school was tough. By now 6-foot-tall (1.8-meter) Maya towered over most of her classmates. They made fun of her size 13 shoes. But her mother had plans for her. She helped Maya focus on her future. Maya researched colleges. She wrote letters and sent out résumés. Her mother also told her that colleges don't just want nice letters. They want good grades and stats. "My mom showed me how important it is to surround yourself with opportunities and make the most of them," said Maya.

Former WNBA star
Cynthia Cooper

FACT

Young Maya's favorite WNBA stars were Cynthia Cooper and Marion Jones.

> Knowing that being a basketball player was okay, as a female, it was cool, it was exciting. You could say, 'I want to be a pro basketball player,' and it was possible. We had a place.
>
> —Maya Moore on watching the WNBA, *Minneapolis City Pages*, July 21, 2016

High School Success

Maya enrolled at Collins Hill High School. By this time she was determined to succeed at everything. And she did. Maya was named to the *USA Today* freshman and sophomore All-America teams. She was back-to-back Naismith National Player of the Year. Her high school team racked up three state titles. In her time there, the team held a 125–3 record.

In 2007 Maya graduated from high school with a 4.0 GPA. She was ready to launch the plan she'd had since middle school — college basketball. If colleges didn't know her name before, they knew it now. Everybody wanted Maya Moore.

FACT

In addition to basketball, Maya was a track and field athlete in high school. She was the state runner-up in the high jump.

Maya playing high school ball in 2007

CHAPTER 3

Driven to Win

Maya chose the University of Connecticut (UConn). She knew Huskie coach Geno Auriemma wouldn't treat her like a star. Together they would review her plays, find her weaknesses, and make her better.

Maya arrived ready to work. Whatever her coaches asked, she delivered times 10. One time the coaches assigned each player a certain number of practice shots per week. Others phoned in their number. Not Maya. She sent a text that broke down her shots. She gave numbers and percentages for shots from 7 feet (2.1 m), 15 feet (4.6 m), the three-point line, and from dribbling.

FACT

While Maya was in middle school, she sent a letter to UConn's Coach Auriemma. He still keeps it in his office drawer.

It was all part of Maya's over-the-top work ethic. Maya knew some students used college as a time to "go crazy." That wasn't Maya's plan. She realized winning would depend on the effort she put into it. "It's how I'm wired," said Maya. "I like to do my best in everything I do."

Maya takes a shot during her first season of play at UConn.

OFF THE COURT

Maya was just as determined when it came to her studies. Even though she was on a basketball scholarship, she wanted to get the best education she could. If she felt uncertain about a subject, she went to study sessions. By test time Maya was ready. She graduated with nearly a 3.7 GPA. She won Academic All-American three times. She was Academic All-American of the Year twice.

Game On!

Maya was a college basketball phenomenon. Officials named her Big East Player of the Year. No freshman, male or female, had ever done that before.

Maya quickly took the lead in points, free throws, rebounds, assists, and steals. One sportscaster compared her lightning-fast steals to the strike of a rattlesnake. Except at 284 milliseconds, Maya was faster than a rattlesnake!

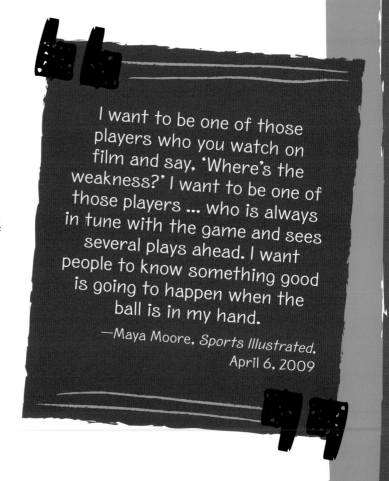

I want to be one of those players who you watch on film and say, 'Where's the weakness?' I want to be one of those players ... who is always in tune with the game and sees several plays ahead. I want people to know something good is going to happen when the ball is in my hand.

—Maya Moore, *Sports Illustrated,* April 6, 2009

Each year the awards piled up. Maya made NCAA All-American four years in a row. She was Wade Trophy winner three times. She was the John R. Wooden Award winner two times. Maya won two NCAA championships with the Huskies in 2009 and 2010. Her remarkable scoring helped the Huskies win the games by big margins. By the time Maya graduated, she did the most impressive thing of all. She helped UConn to a 150–4 record.

Maya with the 2010 NCAA national championship trophy

CHAPTER 4

WNBA Superstar

In 2011 the Minnesota Lynx had the first pick in the WNBA draft. They chose Maya for their team. Now, instead of watching the WNBA players on TV, 22-year-old Maya was one of them. Anyone else might have wanted to take a break and bask in the moment. Not Maya. She never stops.

Maya took the WNBA by storm. She helped lead the Lynx to the best record in the WNBA for the 2011 season. She was also named Rookie of the Year. The Lynx won a playoff series for the first time. Then they went all the way to the WNBA Finals. The Lynx beat the Atlanta Dream at home in the first two games. For game three the Lynx traveled to Atlanta — Maya's hometown. It was another win. The Lynx swept the Dream in three games. Maya had helped them capture their first WNBA title. It had only been five months since she put on a Lynx jersey for the first time.

> It feels really great to finally be able to have the moment of being drafted, going No. 1, and just all the hype and excitement around it. And to see some of the other players that I've grown up competing against and competing with, watching them get drafted as well. . . . I'm really proud to see the quality of players that are in this entire draft. . . . I'm excited to get started this summer.
>
> —Maya Moore to the WNBA after being drafted, April 11, 2011

FACT

The Atlanta Dream play in the same arena where Maya won three straight championships as a high school player.

Maya has played for the Minnesota Lynx since 2011.

Continued Success

Maya hasn't slowed down. She's still racking up awards and wins. Two years after their first WNBA championship, Maya and the Lynx earned their second. Again, they swept the Atlanta Dream in three games. Maya was named Finals MVP. She and the Lynx won WNBA championships in 2015 and 2017 as well.

In 2012 Maya joined Team USA. The team won Olympic gold in London. They won gold again at the 2016 Olympics in Rio de Janeiro. In between Olympic golds, Maya won the 2014 FIBA World Championship with Team USA. She was named the FIBA World Championship MVP.

FACT

Maya plays the position of small forward. Small forwards have been called the "do-everything" players for their teams.

FIBA

FIBA, or International Basketball
Federation, holds the Women's Basketball
World Cup every four years. Since its first tournament
in 1953, the United States has won gold nine times.
Only the Soviet Union, Brazil, and Australia have also
won gold.

Maya celebrates Olympic gold with teammates
Seimone Augustus and Lindsay Whalen.

Euroleague and CBA

Playing for the WNBA has its drawbacks. WNBA players only make a fraction of what NBA players earn. To increase her income, Maya plays for teams overseas during the off-season.

In 2012 Maya brought home the Euroleague title for Spain's Ros Casares. The next year she began playing for the Shanxi Flame in China. She led them to three championships in a row from 2013 to 2015. Her fans call her Invincible Queen.

CHINESE BASKETBALL

Playing basketball in China is fun but challenging. One of the biggest challenges is communicating. "It's pretty comical," said Maya. "I speak English, one of my teammates is Korean. That's two languages. Two of our coaches are Spanish. . . . The first couple of days I was there my head was spinning." During games, the team uses hand signals and numbers. Maya has also learned some basic words in Chinese.

Maya during a 2012 Euroleague game

Winning Ways

It's clear Maya knows how to win. She knows it begins long before she steps on the court. Maya relies on drills. Lots of drills. One important drill is preparing for the last quarter of the game. By then, everyone is tired. Winners have that extra boost of energy to land that last, critical shot. Maya makes sure she is one of them.

Maya spends hours lifting weights. When her body is strong, she's able to avoid common knee and ankle injuries. Diet, ice baths, stretches, and rest are all part of her game plan. "Winning," said Maya, "is not always things people can see."

WINNING AT EVERYTHING

Maya not only wants to win at basketball. She wants to win at *everything*. From card games to silly dance-offs, Maya wants to come out on top. Friends understand that it's just a part of her competitive drive.

Maya during a 2016 practice for the Summer Olympics

CHAPTER 5

Moore to Come

Maya keeps busy off the court too. One highlight was visiting the White House as an NCAA champion and an Olympic gold medalist. She even shot some hoops with President Barack Obama. She's been there so often the president joked about it. He said that Maya should have "her own toothbrush and wing" in the White House.

In 2011 Maya signed a deal with Jordan Brand. She was the first female athlete the popular shoe brand ever signed. A line of shoes would now carry her name. As a result, Maya appeared on the cover of the catalog *Eastbay*. It was a special treat. Maya grew up searching through its pages for news about the latest athletic gear. Now she was on the cover! It was a slam dunk for this "sneakerhead."

FACT

Maya enjoys spending time with family and friends, music, good food, and anything that involves red velvet cake. She even named one of her Jordan sneakers "Red Velvet."

The Minnesota Lynx visited the White House after their 2015 WNBA championship win. The team gave President Barack Obama a Lynx jersey.

Ready for Moore

When she's not racking up more wins and awards, Maya inspires young female basketball players at basketball clinics and sports camps. She helps young players follow their basketball dreams. And her success and example show them how to win at life.

What's next? Maya's options are wide open. Maya has a degree in sports media and promotion. One day she might trade in her basketball for a microphone. Marriage and family are also on her list. Whatever she chooses, Maya will be ready. It's what made her who she is — a basketball superstar!

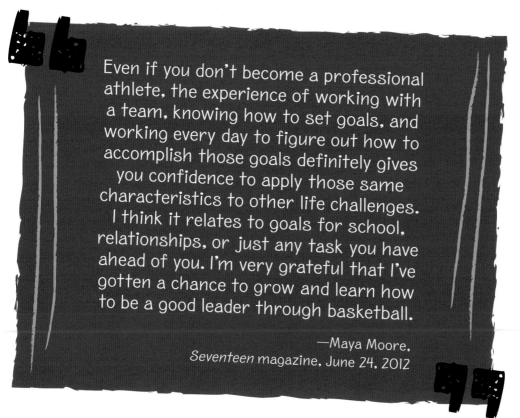

Even if you don't become a professional athlete, the experience of working with a team, knowing how to set goals, and working every day to figure out how to accomplish those goals definitely gives you confidence to apply those same characteristics to other life challenges. I think it relates to goals for school, relationships, or just any task you have ahead of you. I'm very grateful that I've gotten a chance to grow and learn how to be a good leader through basketball.

—Maya Moore,
Seventeen magazine, June 24, 2012

Maya poses with the MVPs from the 2016 Jordan Brand Classic.

Timeline

1989 · · born on June 11 in Jefferson City, Missouri

1997 · · gets first basketball hoop

· · WNBA signs its first players

2007 · · graduates from Collins High Hill School
with 4.0 GPA

· · begins playing for the University of Connecticut

2009 · · wins NCAA championship

2010 · · wins NCAA championship

2011 · · graduates from UConn with a degree in
sports media and promotion

· · top WNBA draft pick; begins playing
for Minnesota Lynx

· · wins WNBA championship

· · named WNBA Rookie of the Year

2012 · · plays for Spain's Ros Casares; wins Euroleague title

· · joins Team USA; wins gold medal at Olympics
in London

2013 · · wins WNBA title and is named WNBA Finals MVP

· · begins playing for China's Shanxi Flame

2014 · · named WNBA MVP

· · wins FIBA World Championship and named
FIBA World Championship MVP

2015 · · wins WNBA championship

· · named WNBA All-Star Game MVP

2016 · · Gold medalist at 2016 Olympics in Rio de Janeiro

2017 · · wins WNBA championship against the Los Angeles
Sparks

Read More

Ervin, Phil. *Maya Moore: WNBA Champion*. Playmakers. Minneapolis: Sportszone, 2016.

Raum, Elizabeth. *Maya Moore*. Pro Sports Biographies. Mankato, Minn.: Amicus High Interest, 2018.

Rissman, Rebecca. *Top Basketball Tips*. Top Sports Tips. North Mankato, Minn.: Capstone Press, 2017.

Internet Sites

Use FactHound to find Internet sites related to this book.

Visit *www.facthound.com*

Just type in 9781515797098 and go!

Check out projects, games and lots more at
www.capstonekids.com

Index